Dean's Team

A Division of The McGraw·Hill Companies

Columbus, Ohio

www.sra4kids.com

SRA/McGraw-Hill

A Division of The **McGraw·Hill** *Companies*

Send all inquiries to:
SRA/McGraw-Hill
8787 Orion Place
Columbus, OH 43240-4027

ISBN 0-07-569926-5
5 6 7 8 9 DBH 05

Kenny and Dad hurried to see Dean
play. The Mean Streaks are Dean's team.
"The Mean Streaks are really neat,"
says Kenny.

Dean is the pitcher, and Dad's niece, Kay,
is the catcher.
Dean hurls the pitch.

Jim is the batter. He swings and misses.
"Sweet pitch, Dean!" yells Kenny.

Steve, Jeanie, and Becky play the
three bases.
Pete plays between second and third.
"A perfect catch! Three cheers for Pete!"
yells Kenny.

Gena, Kareem, and Kelly are in the field.
The pitch speeds past Pete.

Gena reaches up and grabs it.

"She is fantastic!" yells Kenny. "See what I mean, Dad? These Mean Streaks cannot be beat!"